Jos Hendriks

Math Art
for the coffee table

uniform star patterns

2014

Hendriks en Hendriks

Editors: Luuk de Weert, Matt Wagner, Jos Hendriks
Cover design Luuk de Weert

ISBN: 978-90-821900-0-7

For Luuk, Marian and René

Introduction

Place this book on your coffee table, near your couch or beside your bed for those moments when you want to drift off and immerse yourself in something special. It's not only for yourself of course, but also for your family, friends or whoever happens to be around. Everyone can pick up this book and admire these intriguingly beautiful, yet simple patterns.

This edition contains 83 page-wide plates. All of them are in full color.

You may find it surprising that all the patterns in this book, also known as tilings, are comprised of just a few shapes, seamlessly fitted together. The shapes are no more than regular polygons and regular stars. You can see all the shapes that are used, sometimes referred to as "tiles" on page 90.

The patterns are essentially decorative and can be extended as far as you want. There are repetitions in two directions and a small part contains all the information used in the whole pattern. On pages 91-96 you can see these minimal parts. Together with these minimal parts, there is information about the kinds of polygons used for each pattern and how one pattern can be derived from another. This information is useful not only if you simply want to admire the patterns but also if you want to use them in a project of you own. In a few patterns, some of the polygons are filled in with a rosette, which lets you see further possibilities for developing the patterns. The rosettes gives the patterns the same distinctive look and feel as that found in Islamic Art. Generally speaking, when you decorate patterns such as those found in this book in this way, they stay more regular.

I call this art "math art" because the forms used are well-defined mathematical objects: regular polyhedra and regular stars. Because there are several different definitions for regular stars, I show you on page 90 what is meant by this term in this book. The tilings were basically found using trial and error. I had just a few rules of thumb. For example, it is well known that there are exactly fifteen ways to position regular polygons around one point. You can see them all on page 90. As a starting point I also used a classification of tilings by looking at the different situations existing around the points where the tiles meet. Joseph Meyers enumerates all the tilings where the situation is the same for all points in an article, which you can download here:

http://www.kleurrijkewiskunde.nl/downloads/star-polygon-tiling.pdf

He also enumerates the tilings with two different situations at the points where the tiles meet. To download the article with these results, see

http://www.kleurrijkewiskunde.nl/downloads/star-polygon-tiling-2-uniform.pdf

He missed (at least) one possibility, which I myself stumbled upon and which you can see on plate XLI.

I sincerely hope you will have as much pleasure looking at these designs as I had in creating them.

The author

Plate I

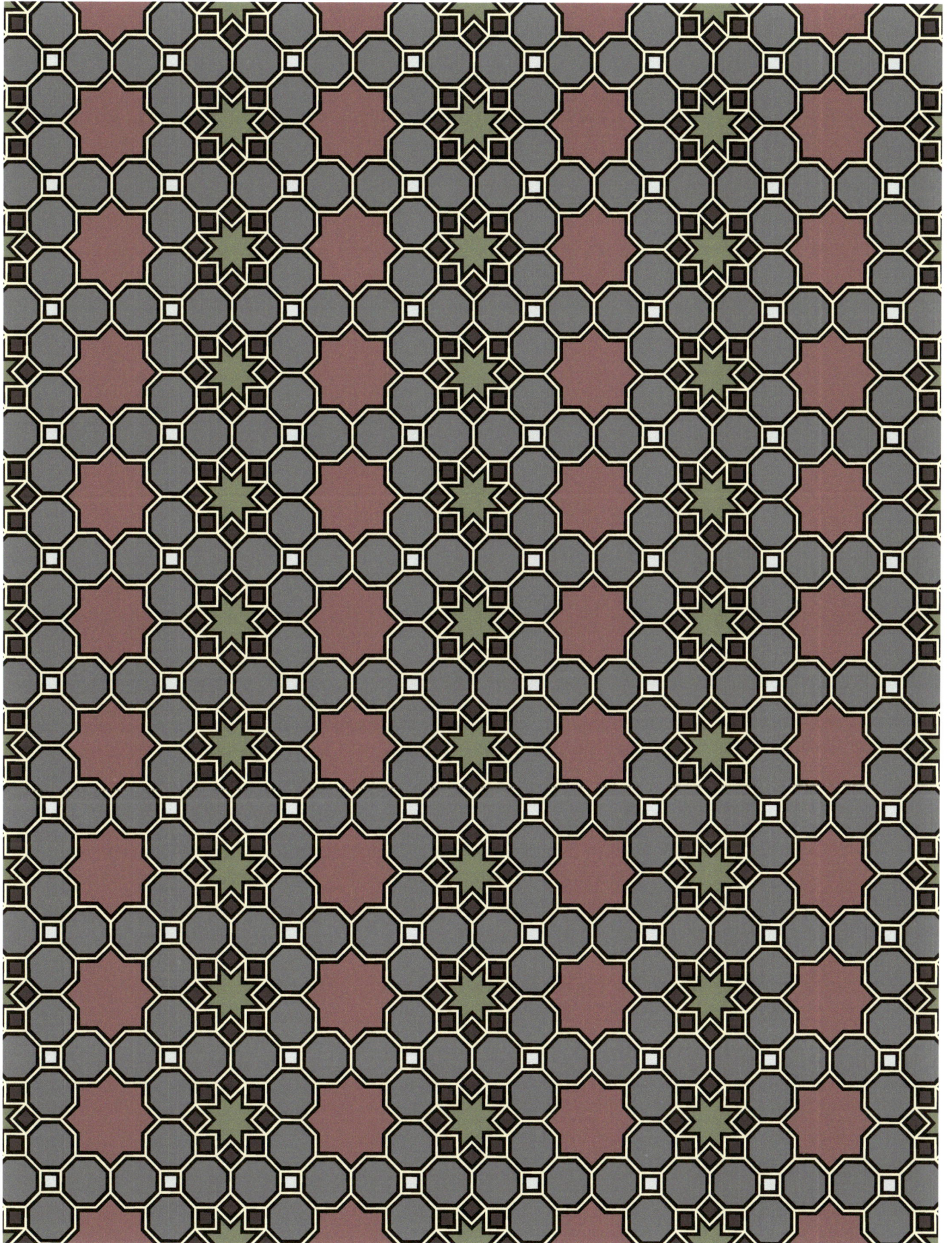

Plate II

Plate III

Plate IV

Plate V

Plate VI

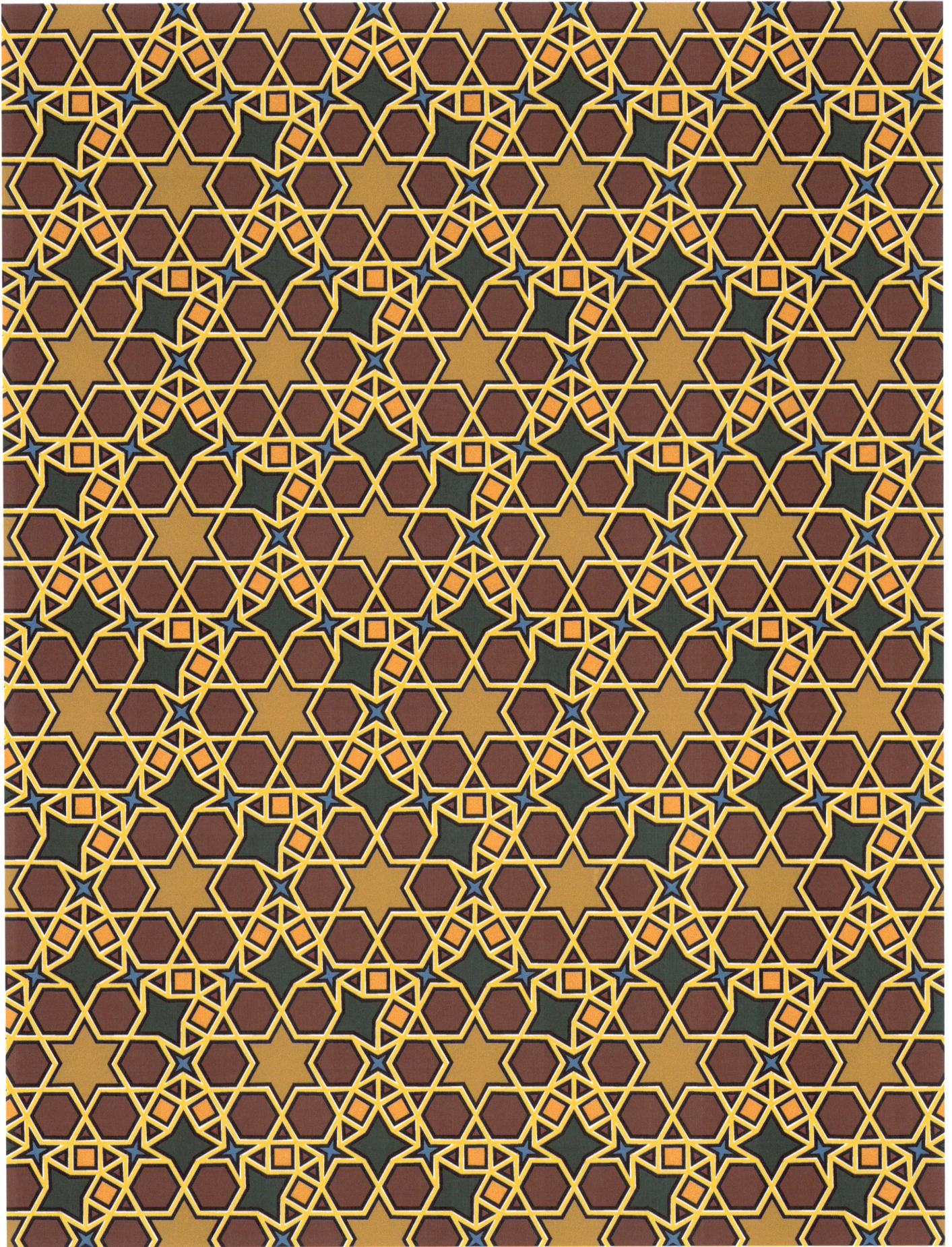

Plate VII

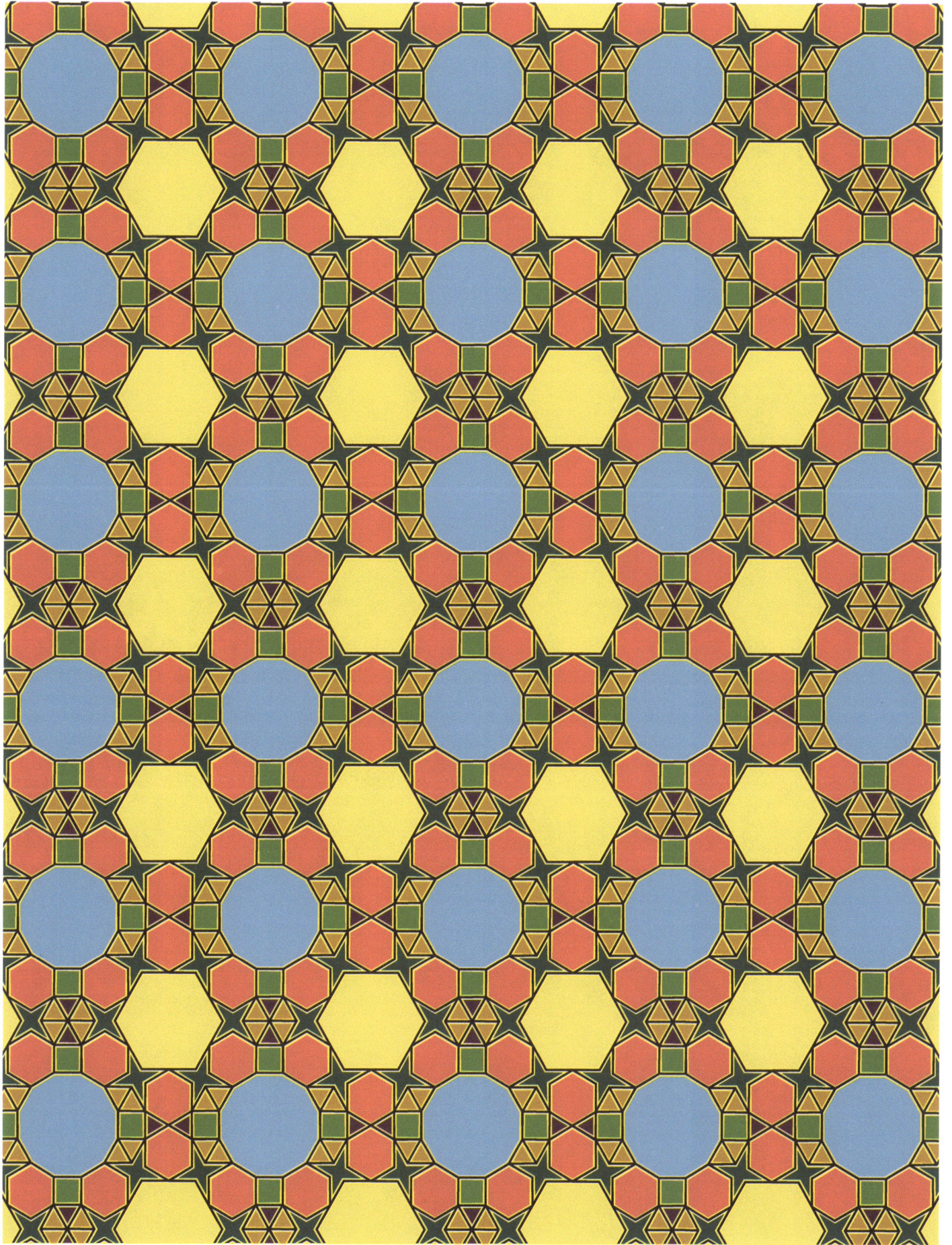

Plate VIII

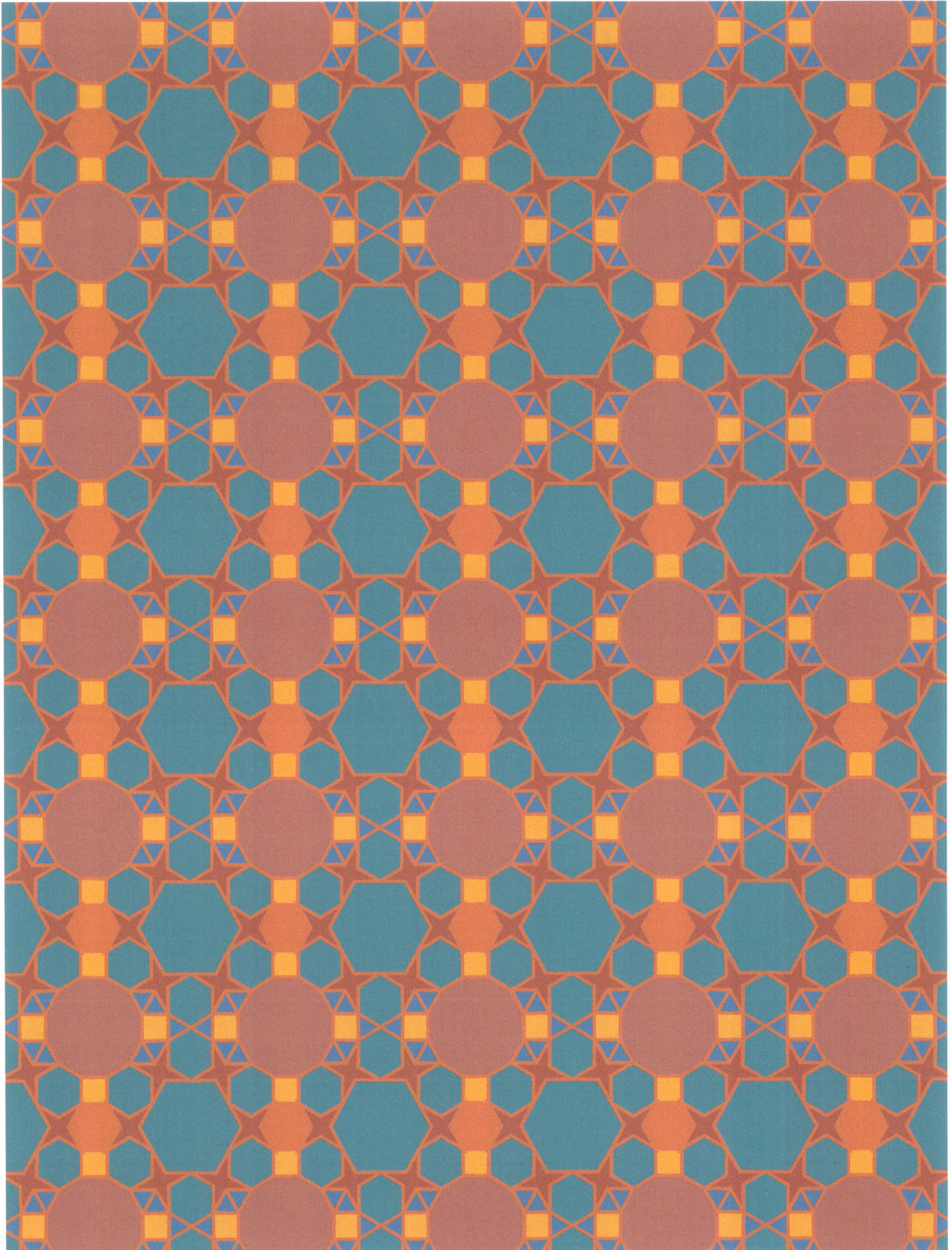

Plate XI

Plate X

Plate XI

Plate XII

Plate XIII

Plate XIV

Plate XV

Plate XVI

Plate XVII

Plate XVIII

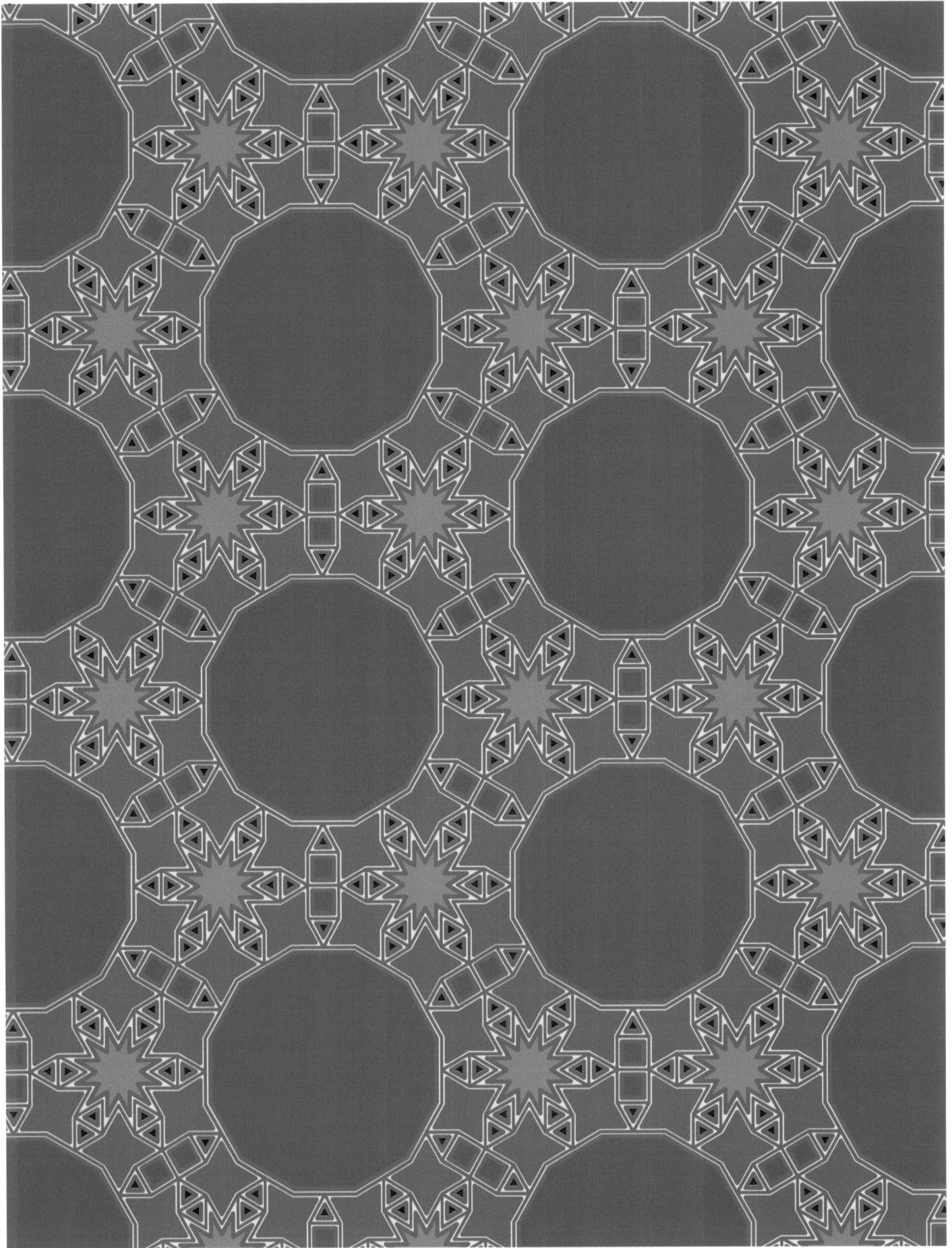

Plate XIX

Plate XX

Plate XXI

Plate XXII

Plate XXIII

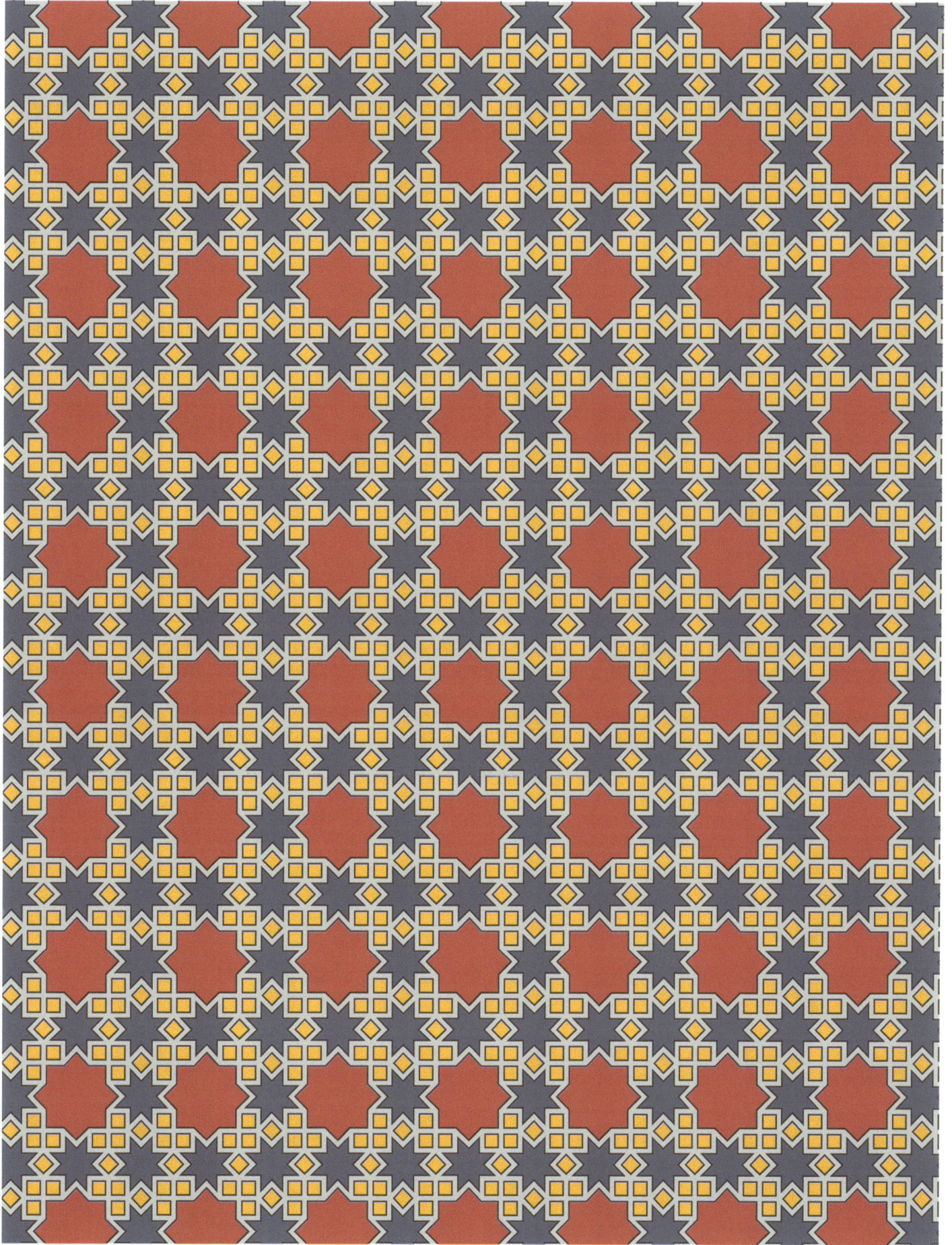

Plate XXIV

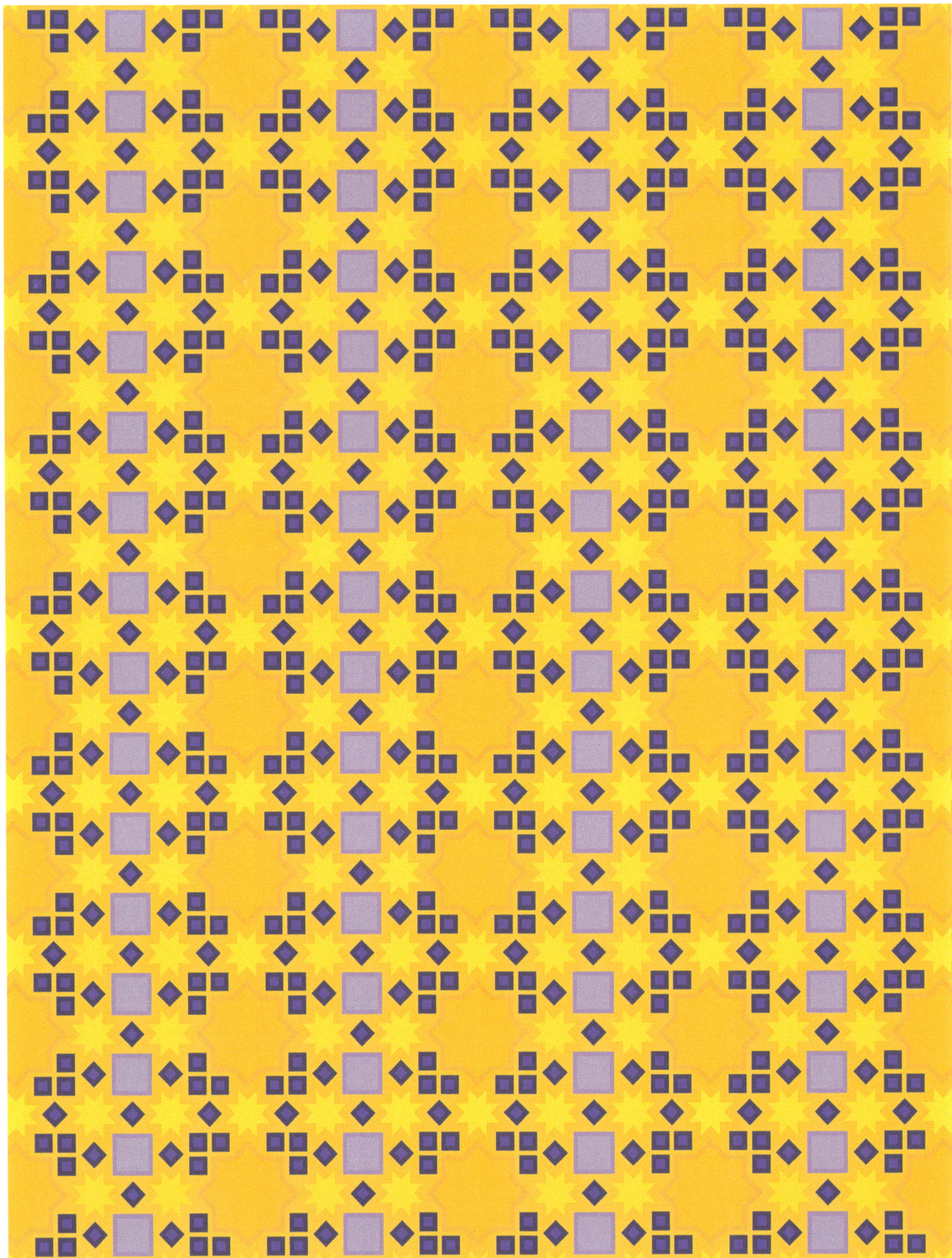

Plate XXV

Plate XXVI

Plate XXVII

Plate XXVIII

Plate XIX

Plate XXX

Plate XXXI

Plate XXXII

Plate XXXIII

Plate XXXIV

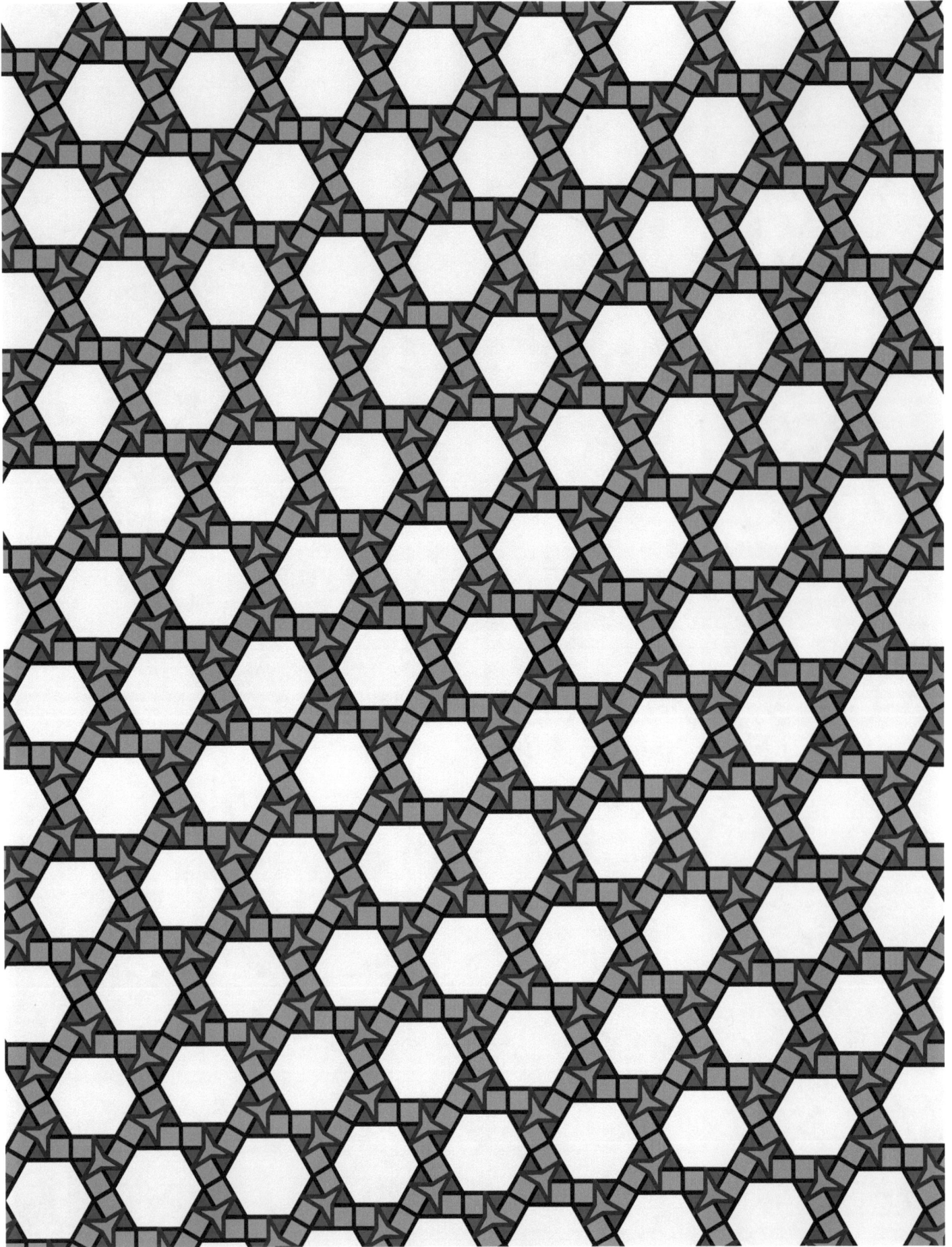

Plate XXXV

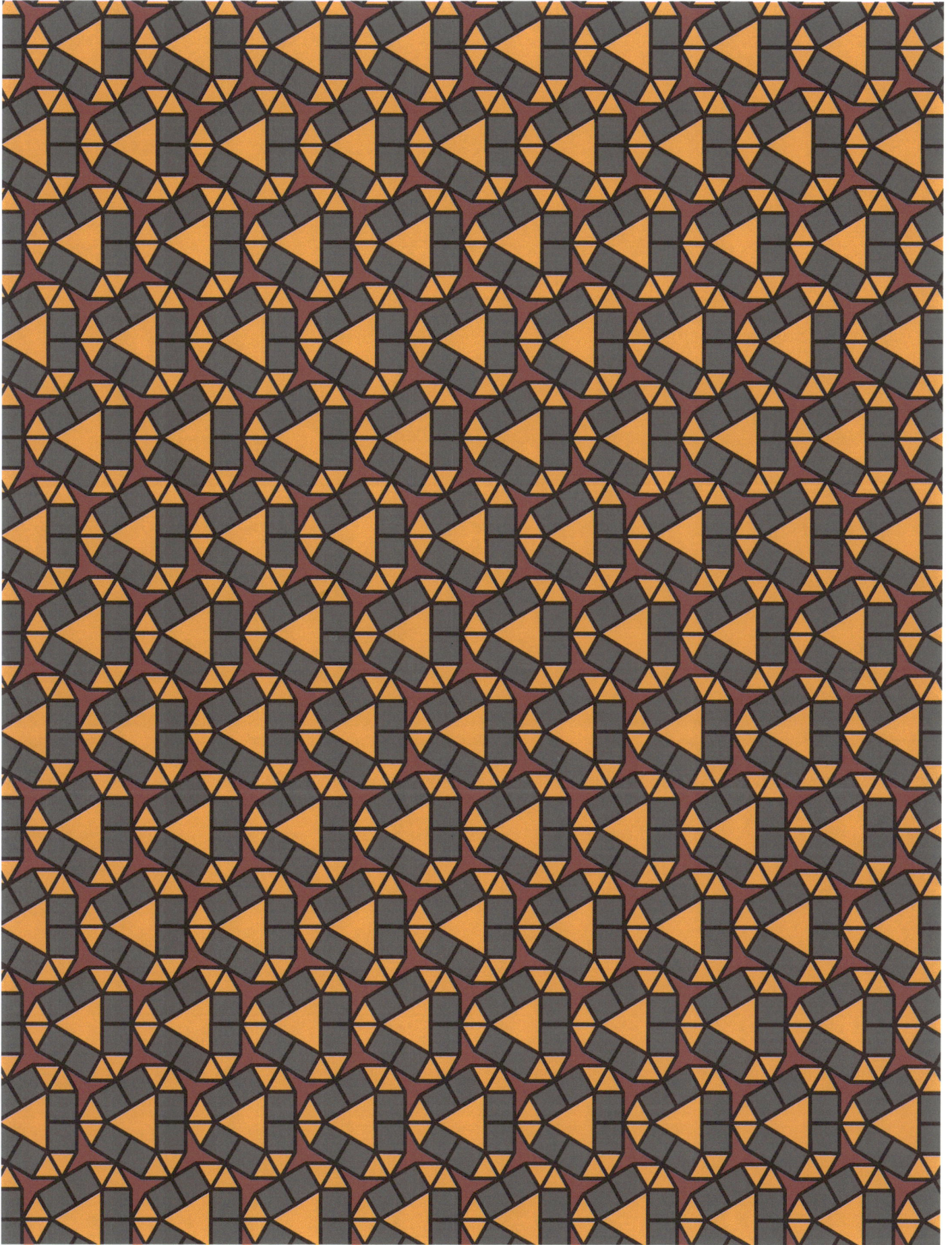

Plate XXXVI

Plate XXXVII

Plate XXXVIII

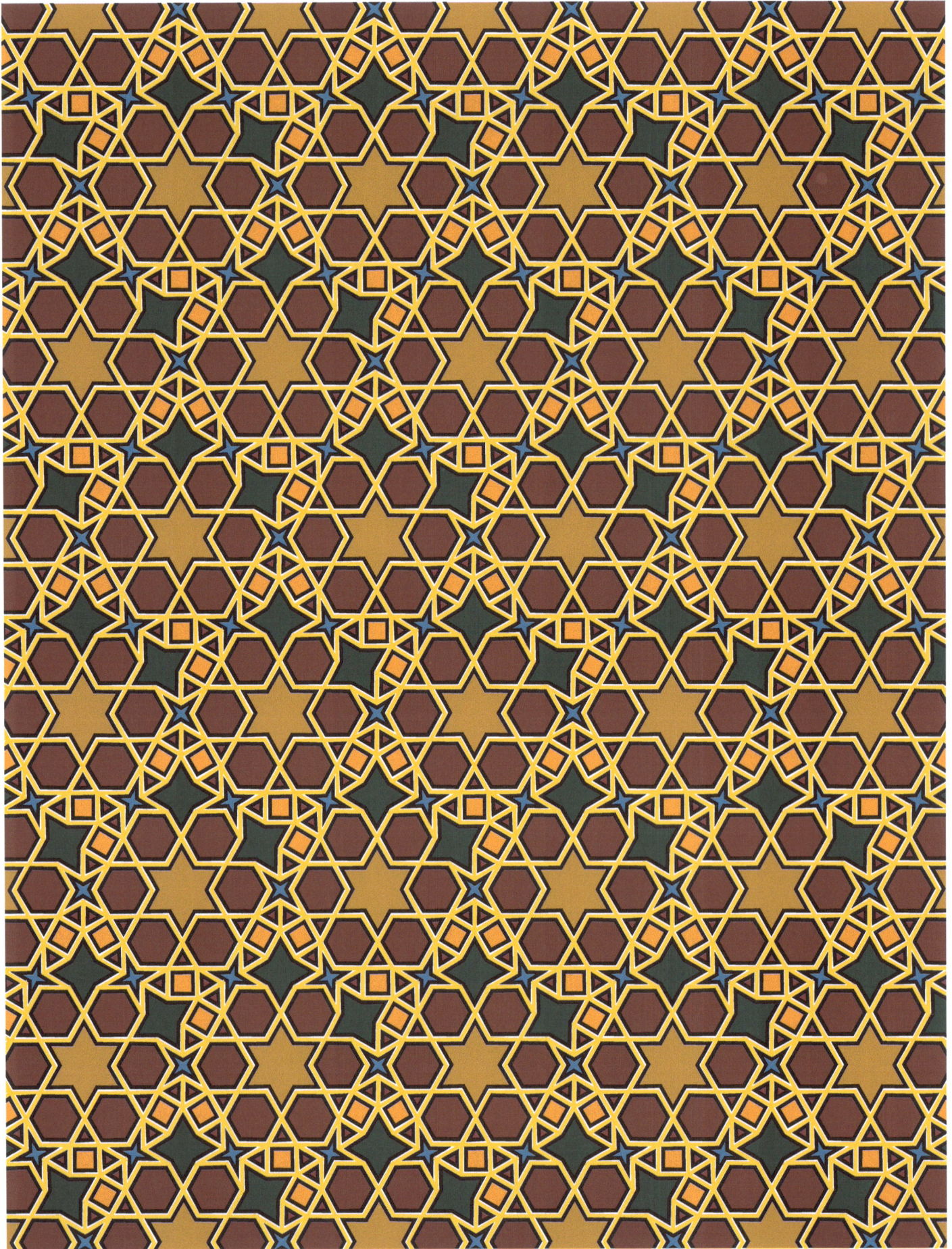

Plate XXXIX

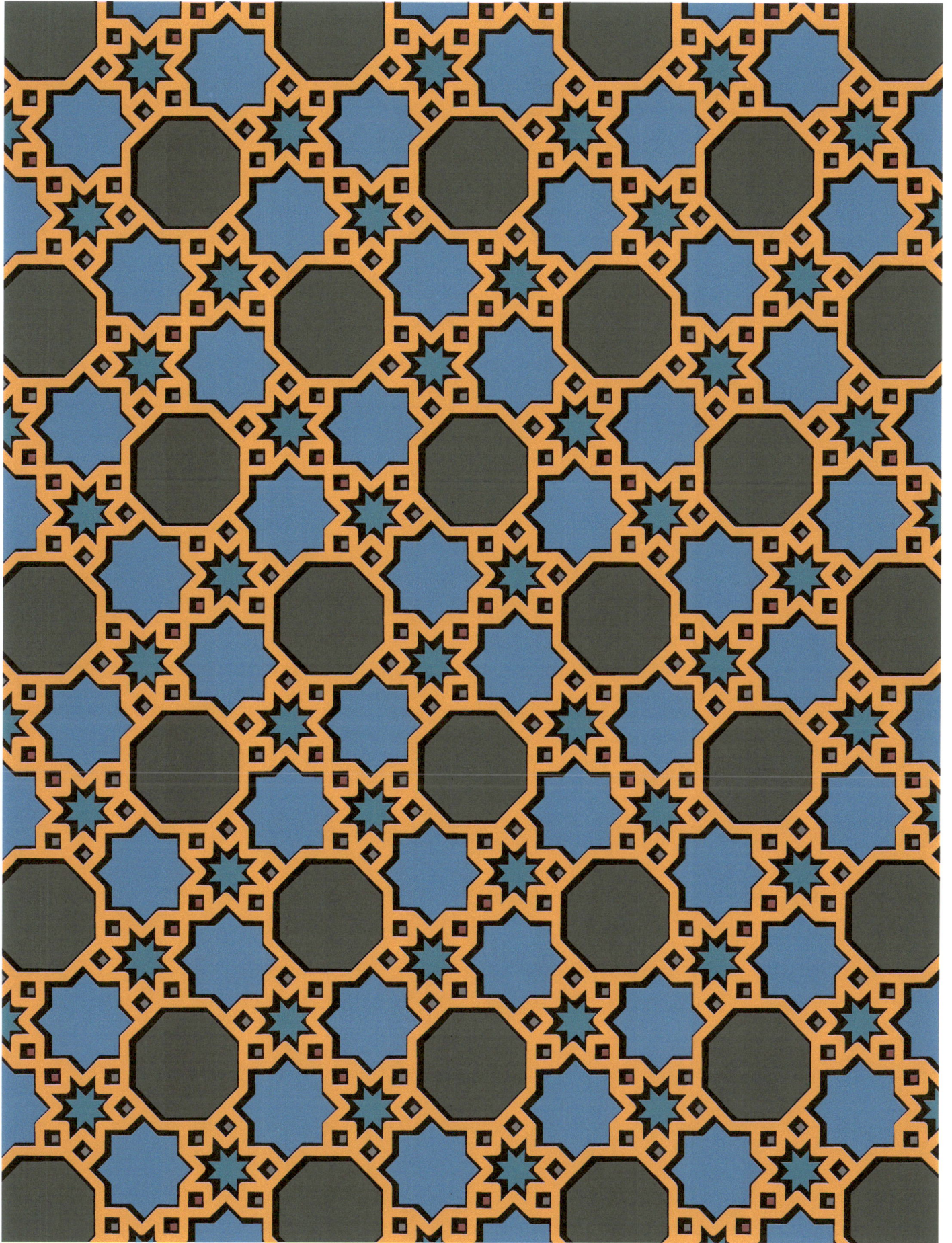

Plate XL

Plate XLI

Plate XLII

Plate XLIII

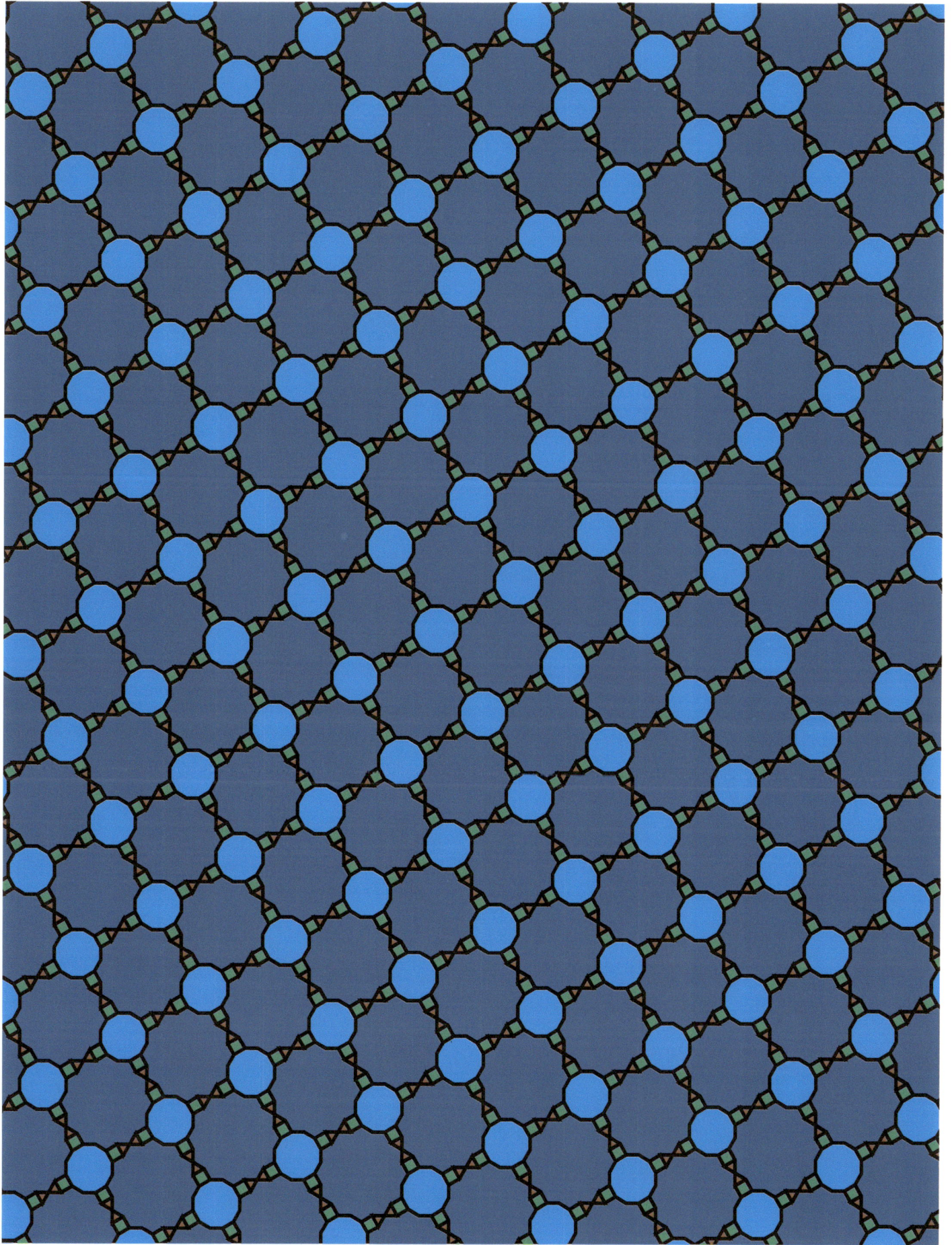

Plate XLIV

Plate XLV

Plate XLVI

Plate XLVII

Plate XLVIII

Plate XLIX

Plate L

Plate LI

Plate LII

Plate LIII

Plate LIV

Plate LV

Plate LVI

Plate LVII

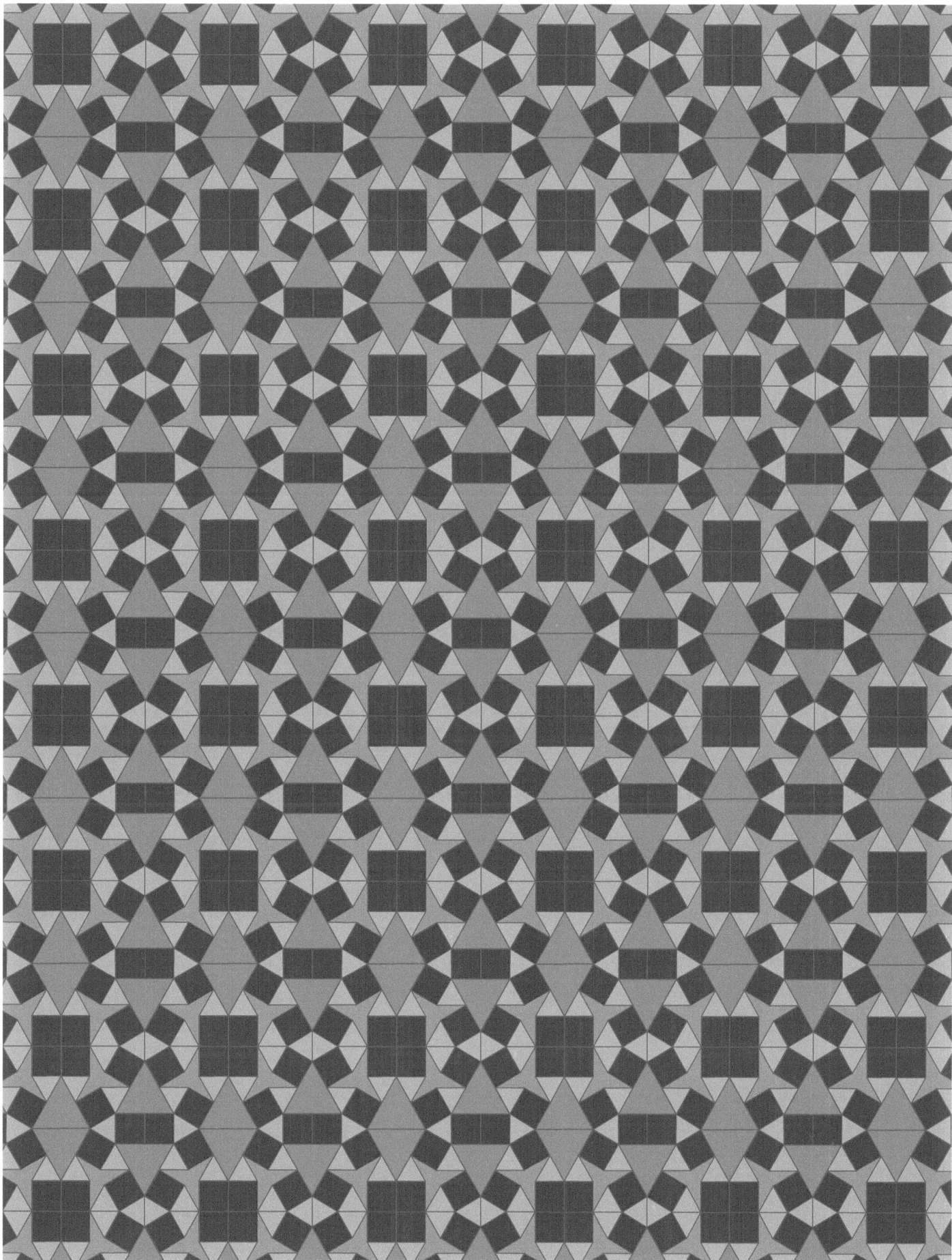

Plate LVIII

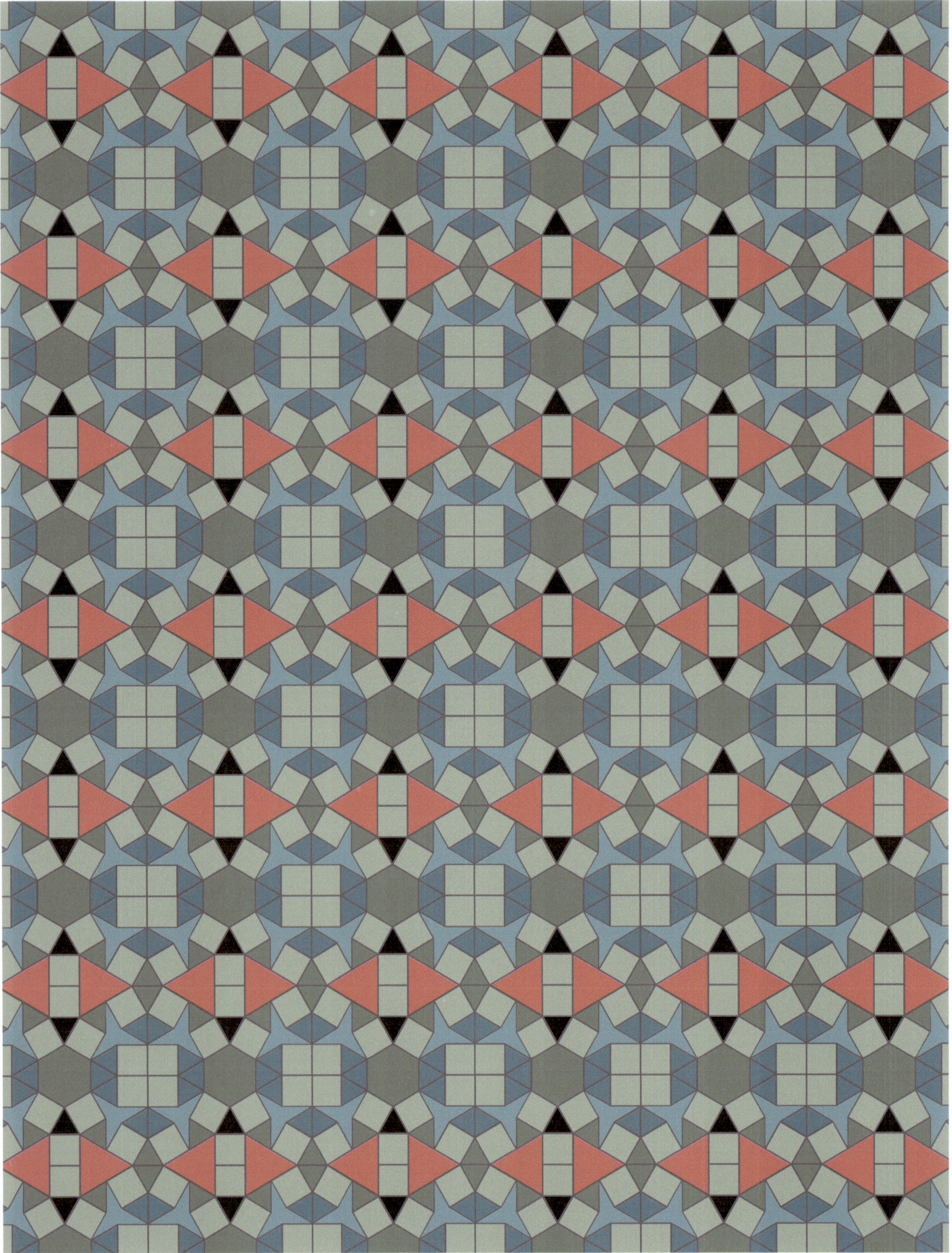

Plate LIX

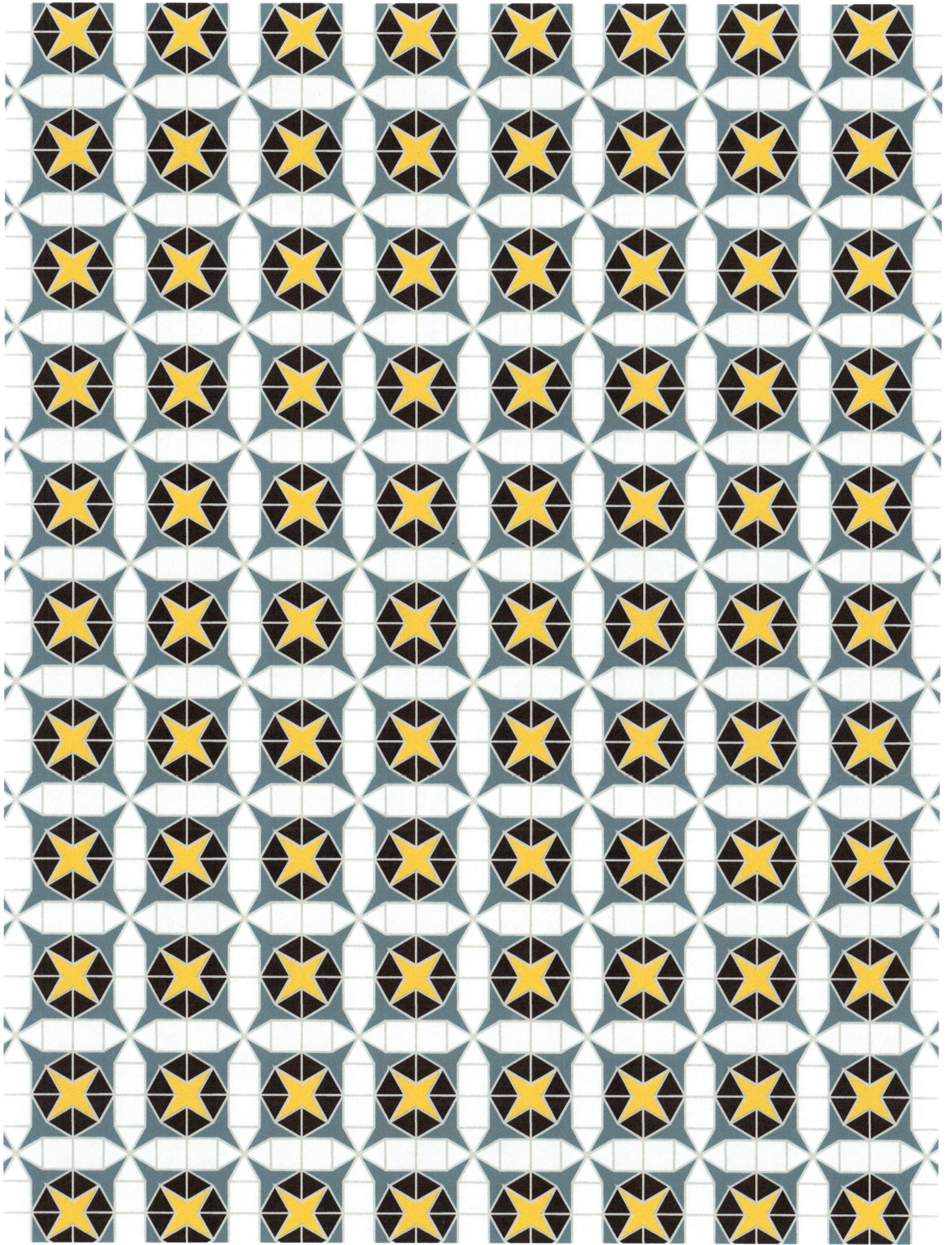

Plate LX

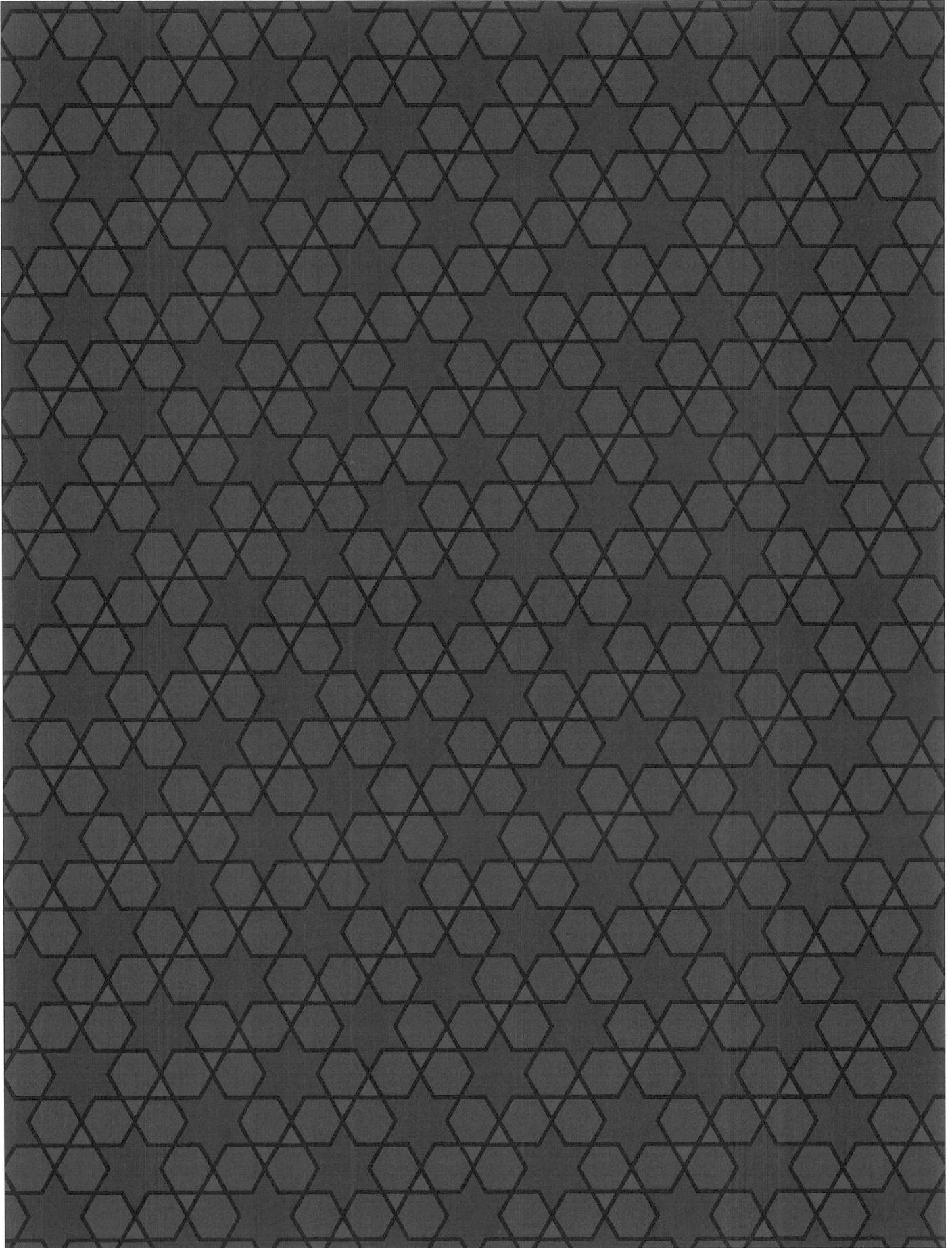

Plate LXI

Plate LXII

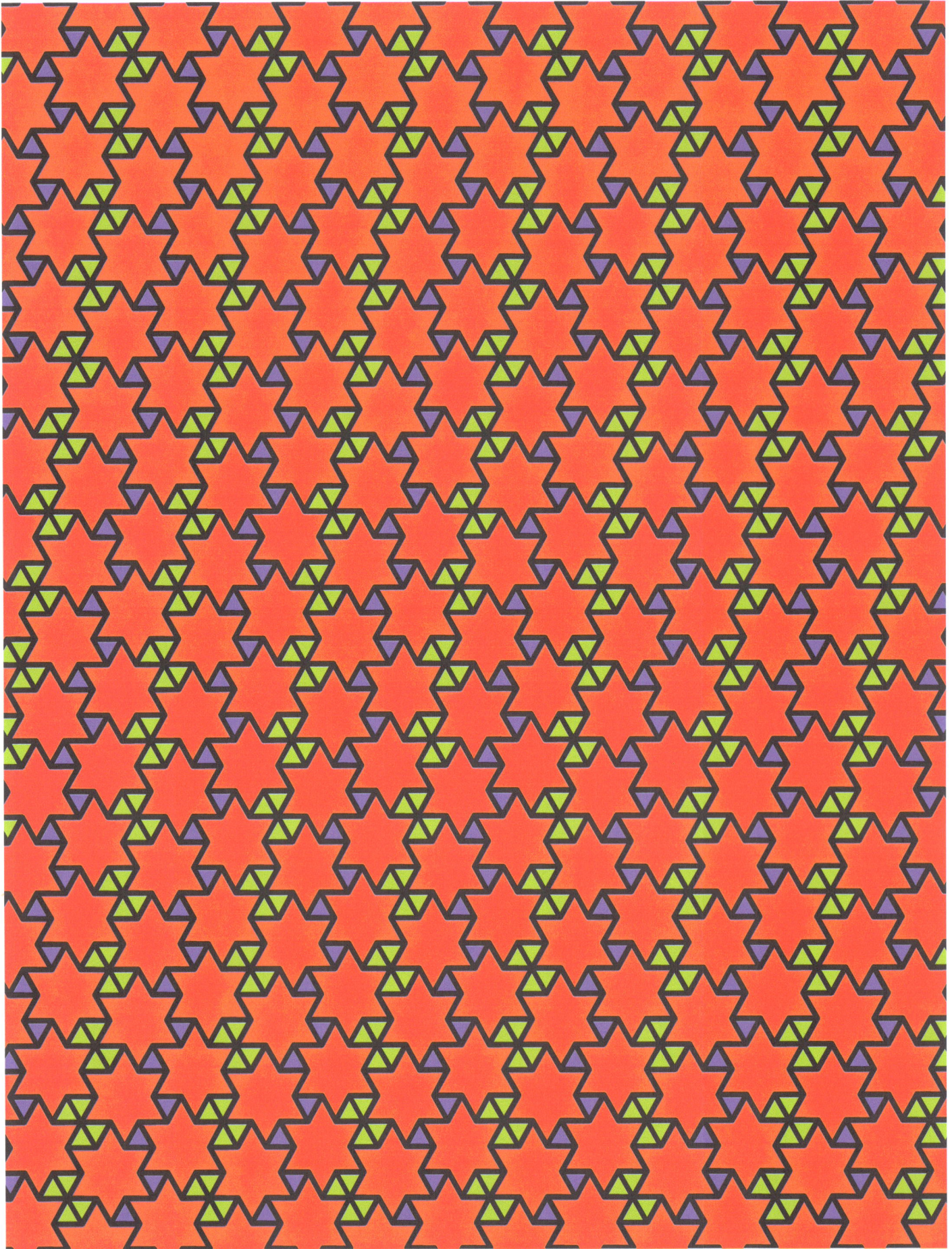

Plate LXIII

Plate LXIV

Plate LXV

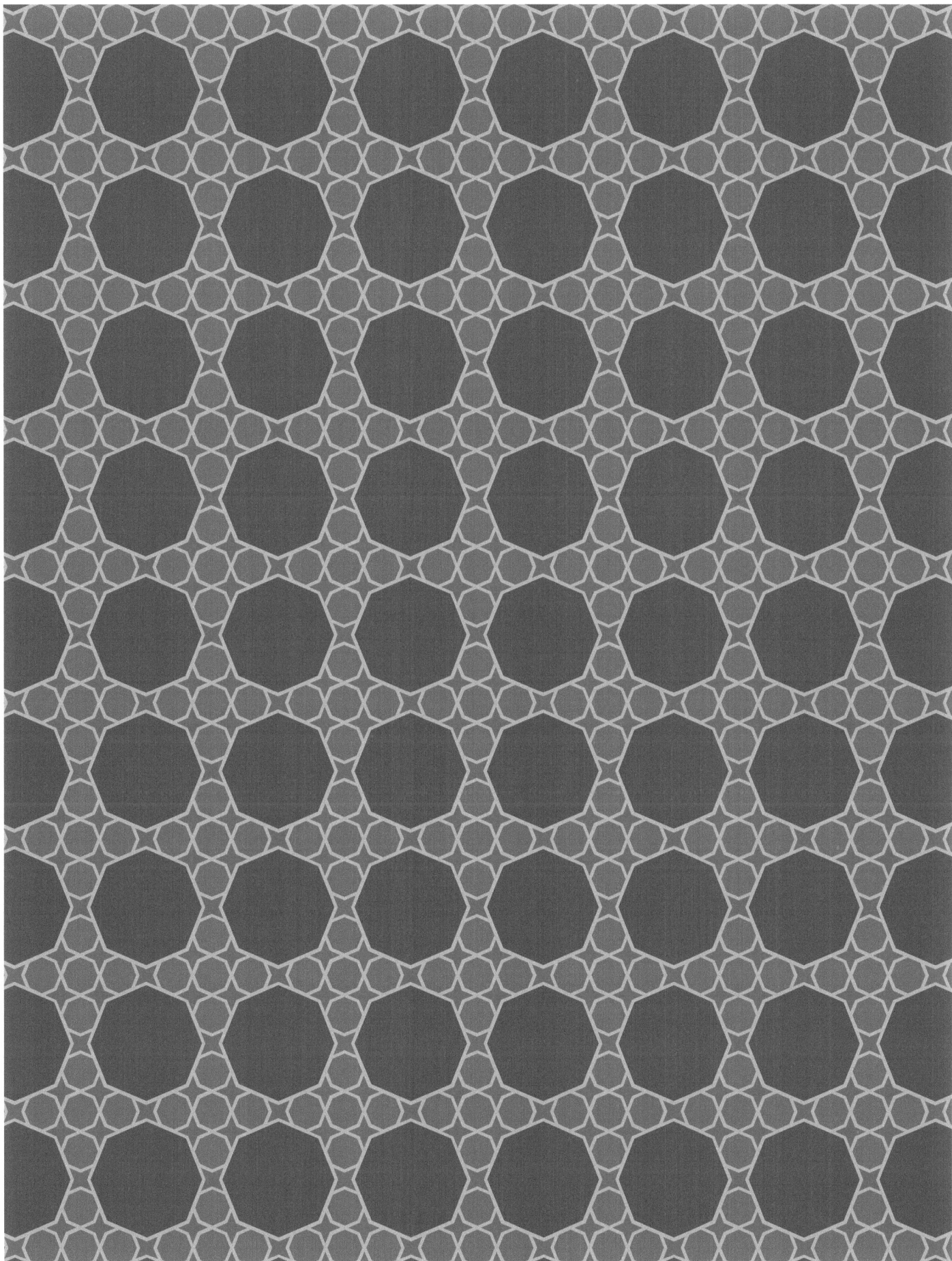

Plate LXVI

Plate LXVII

Plate LXVIII

Plate LXIX

Plate LXX

Plate LXXI

Plate LXXII

Plate LXXIII

Plate LXXIV

Plate LXXV

Plate LXXVI

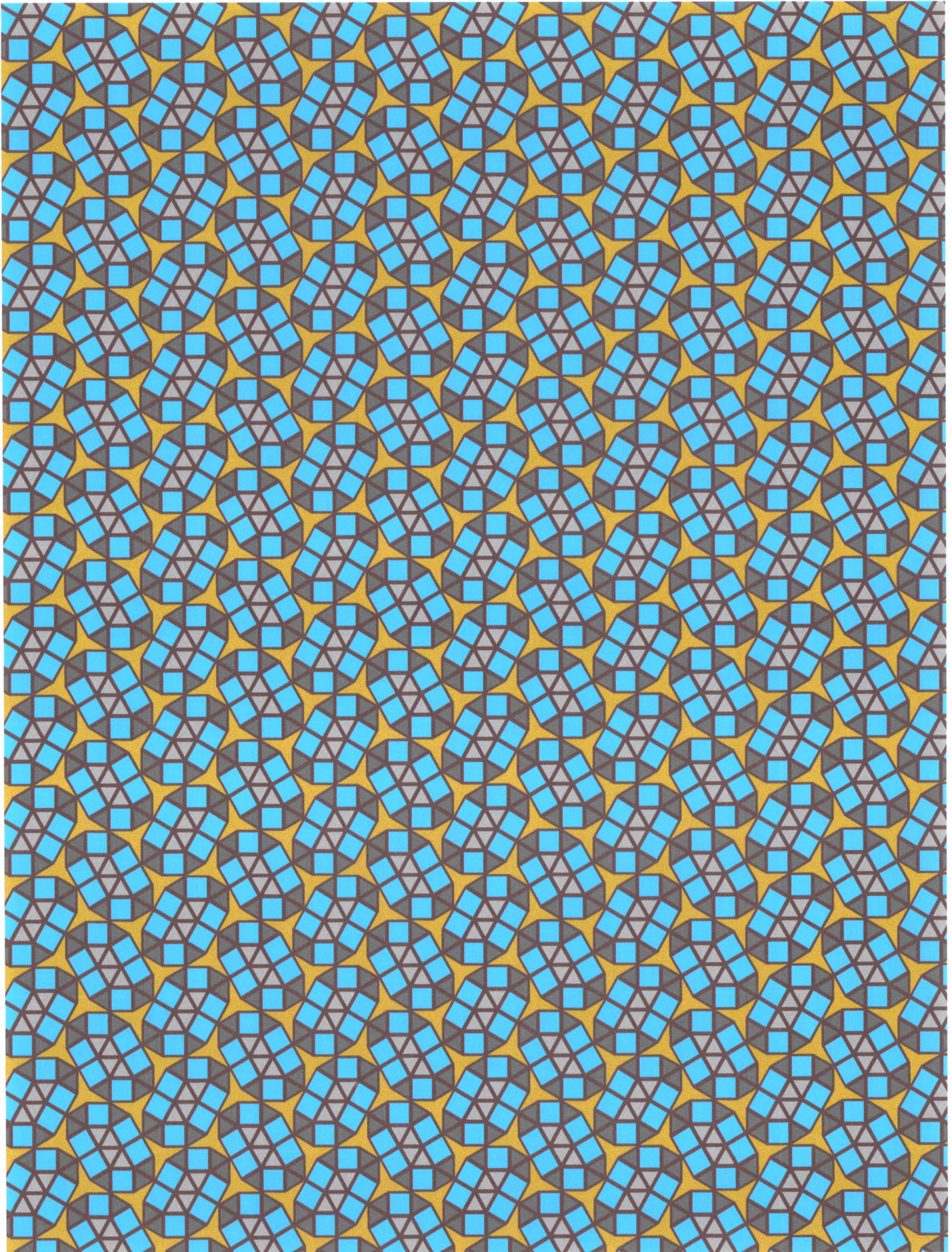

Plate LXXVII

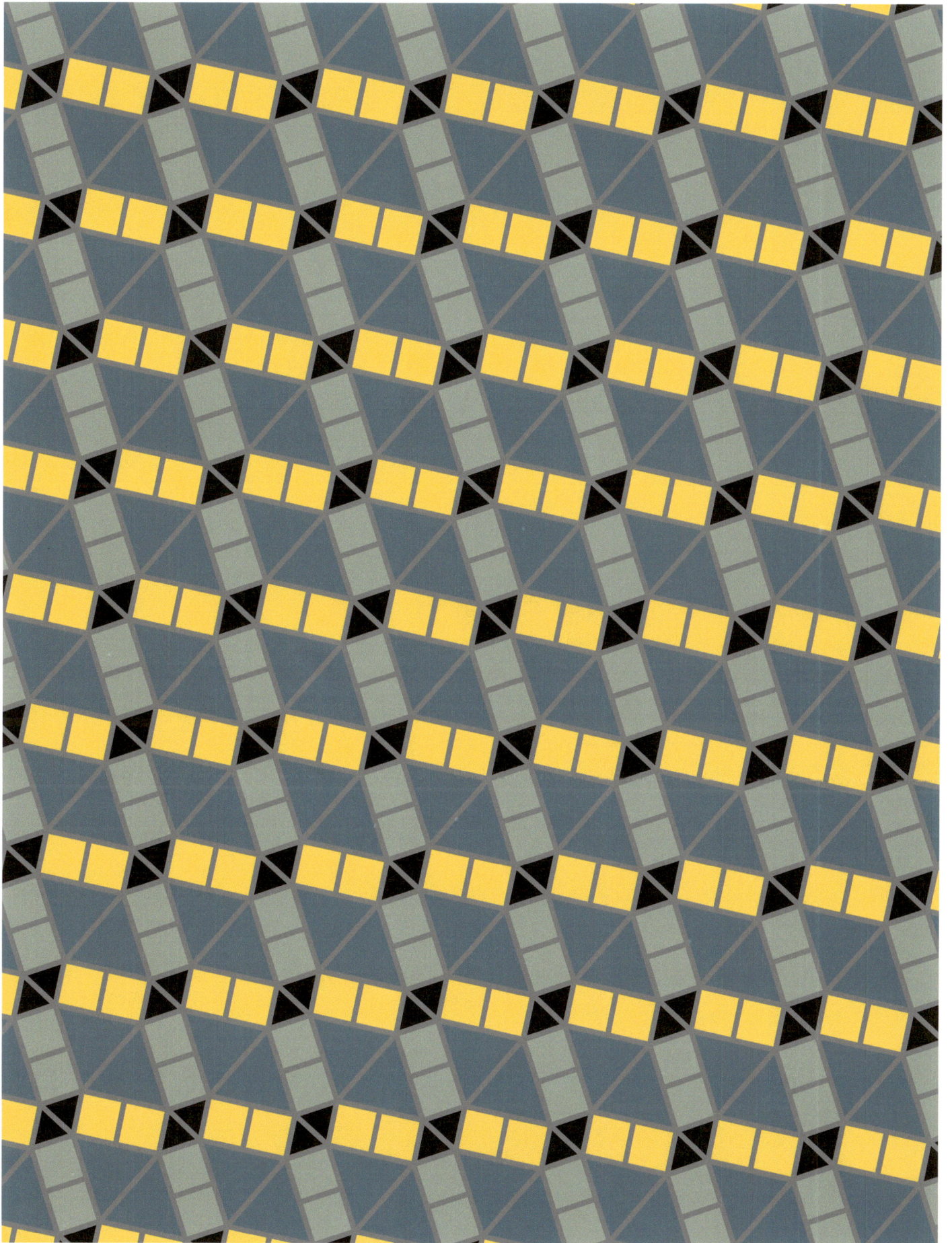

Plate LXXVIII

Plate LXXIX

Plate LXXX

Plate LXXXI

Plate LXXXII

Plate LXXXIII

Explanatory drawings and notes

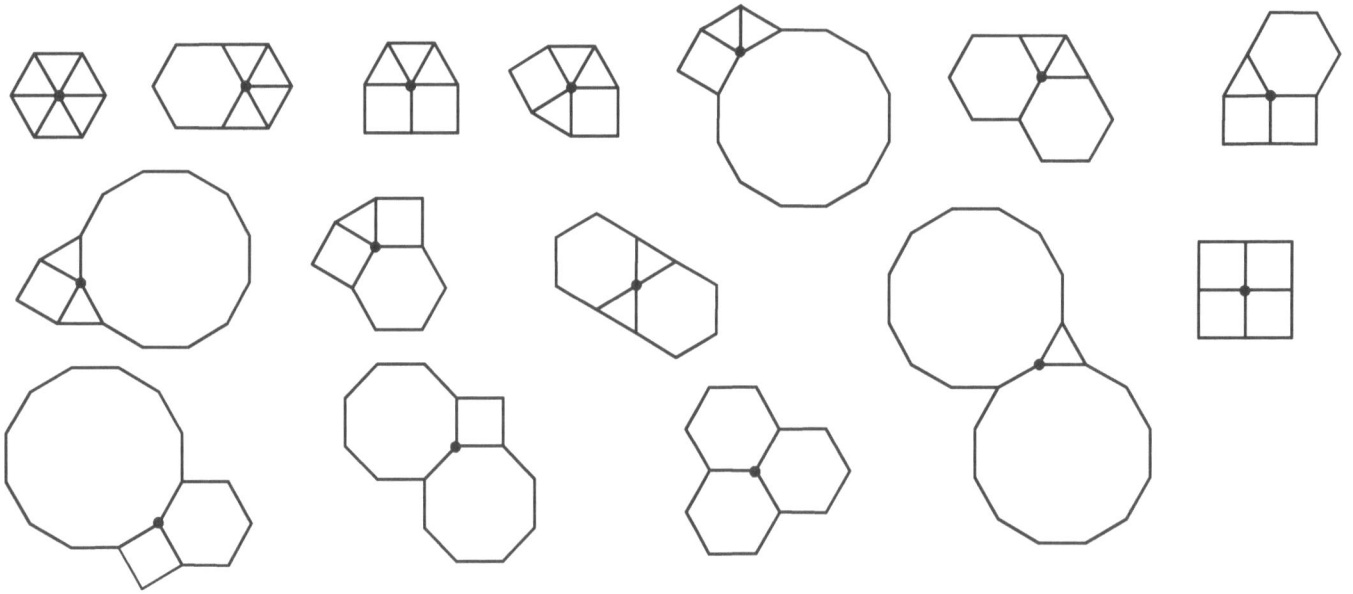

The fifteen possibilities for arranging regular polygons around a point without leaving a gap.

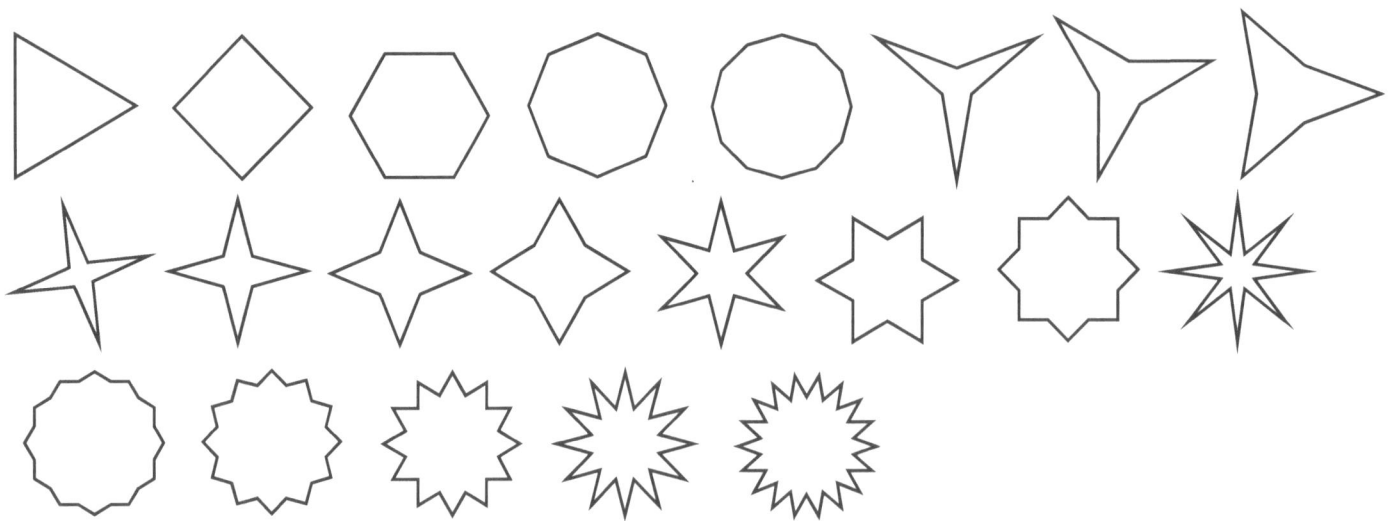

These are the only parts used in the patterns.

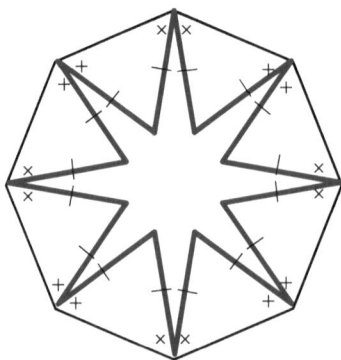

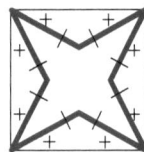

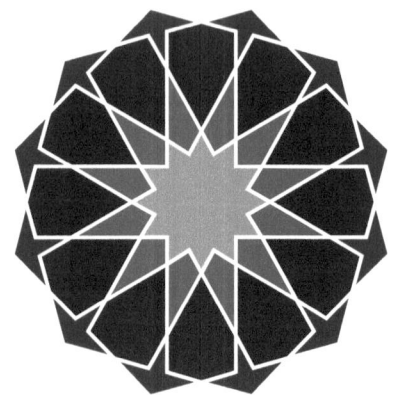

Every construction of equal isosceles triangles
on the sides of a regular polygon yields a regular star.

In a few patterns dodecahedral
stars are filled in with this rosette.

Plate I

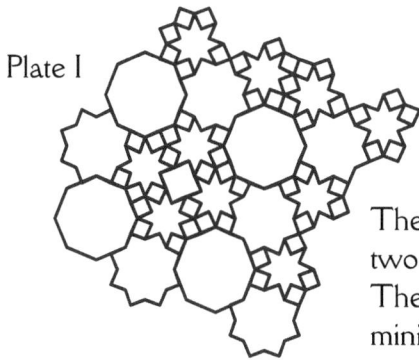

When we speak of a triangle, we always mean a regular triangle. The same goes for other parts. For instance, by octagon we mean a regular octagon and by a 4-pointed star, a regular star.

The patterns of plate I, II and III consist of octahedra, squares, and two different octahedral stars with angles of 90 degrees and 45 degrees. The repeating part of plate I consist of 73 tiles. Those for Plate II and III use a minimal part of 20 tiles to repeat.

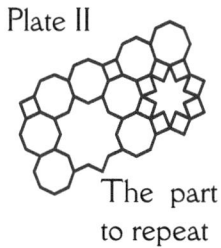

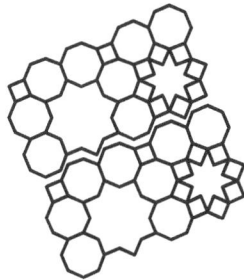

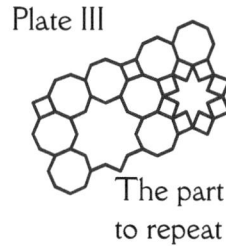

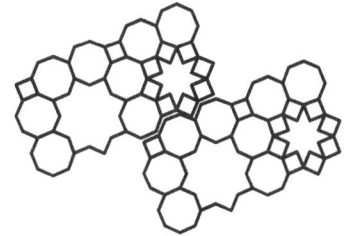

Plate II

The part to repeat

Plate III

The part to repeat

The part to repeat for plate II and plate III is the same, but combining these parts in different ways yields different patterns.

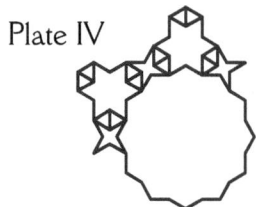

Plate IV

Triangles, 4-, 6- and 12-pointed stars. 18 parts to repeat. In the pattern the 12-pointed stars are filled in with rosettes.

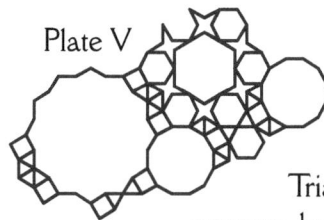

Plate V

Triangles, squares, hexagons and decagons, 4- and 12- pointed stars,

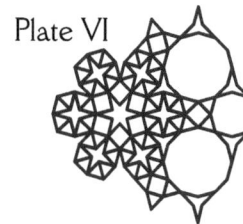

Plate VI

Triangles, squares, dodecagons, 3- 4- and 6-pointed stars, the region to repeat has 84 parts.

Plate VII

The region to repeat has 28 parts: 12 triangles, 4 squares, 6 hexagons, three 4- pointed stars with an angle of 30 and two 3-pointed stars with an angle of 60 degrees and one 6- pointed star.

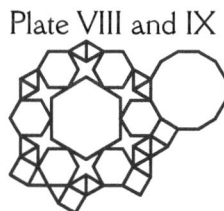

Plate VIII and IX

34 Parts: 16 triangles, 4 squares, 7 hexagons in 2 seizes, 1 dodecagon and six 4- pointed stars. Notice how the coloring determines the result.

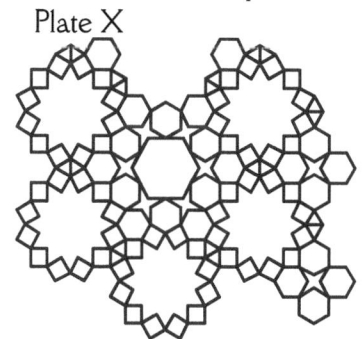

Plate X

The part to repeat exist of 116 tiles.

Plate XI

The difference between the two pictures comes from coloring some edges the same as the interior of the tile.

Plate XII

20 Triangles, two 4-pointed stars.

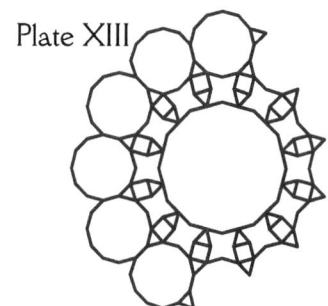

Plate XIII

Plate XIV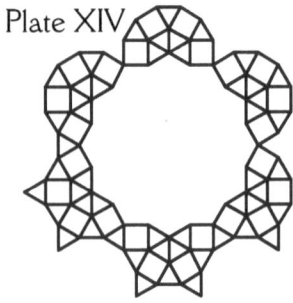

Plate XV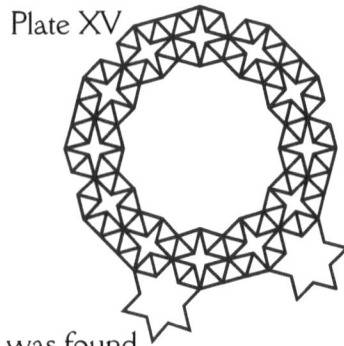

Plate XVI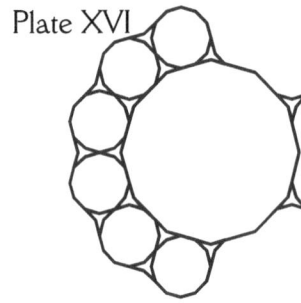

Plate XVII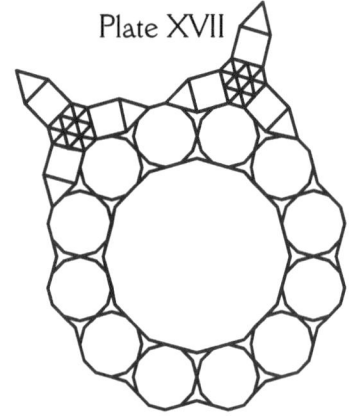

The pattern in Plate XVIII was found by enlarging the minimal part of Plate XV. In the same way the pattern in Plate XVII was found. Here the minimal part of the pattern in Plate XVI has been enlarged.

Plate XVIII

Plate XXII 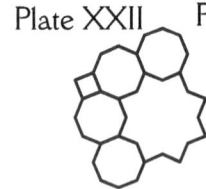 Plate XXI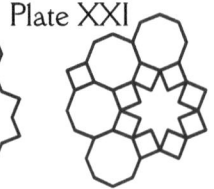

There are several star polygons that can be filled in with other polygons in order to yield different tilings.

Plate XIX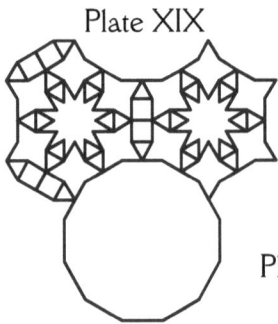

Plate XXIII  Plate XXIV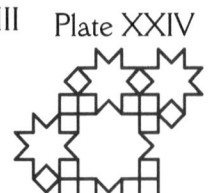

Plate XX

206 tilings

XXIII until XXVI are derived one after the other,

Plate XXV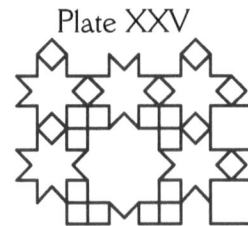

Plate XXVI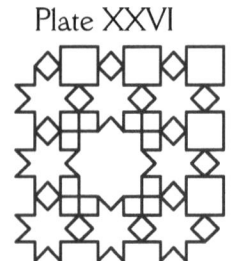

Plate XXVIII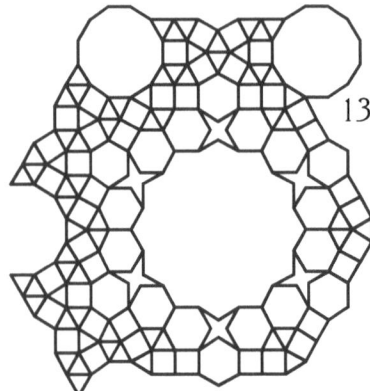

135 tilings to repeat

Plate XXVII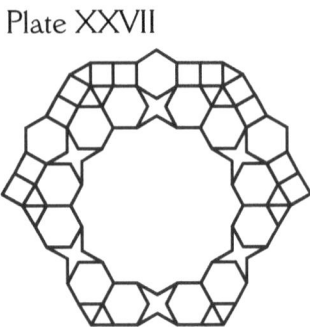

Plate XXIX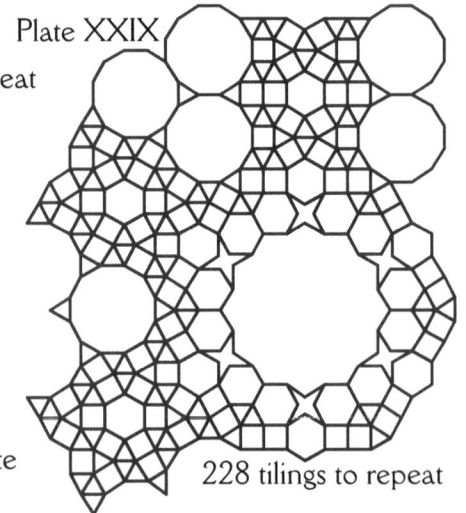

228 tilings to repeat

The pattern in plate XXVIII is the same as the pattern in plate XXVII but with an extra strip of triangles, squares and dodecagons around the star dodecahedron. The pattern in plate XXIX is the same as the pattern in plate XXVIII again with the same kind of extra strip.

92

Plate XXX

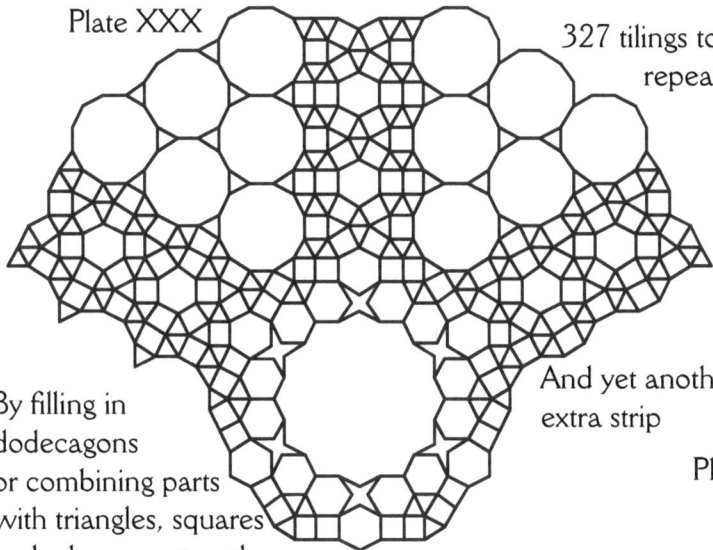

327 tilings to repeat

By filling in dodecagons or combining parts with triangles, squares and a hexagon together, you can create many other patterns.

And yet another extra strip

Plate XXXI

Plate XXXII

Plate XXXIII

Plate XXXV

Plate XXXIV

Plate XXXVI

These four tilings XXXIII-XXXVI are found starting with a triangle, a square and a three pointed star with one angle of 150 degrees so that the triangle and square fit.

Plate XXXVII

Plate XXXVIII

Plate XXXIX

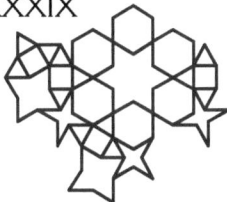

Plate XL

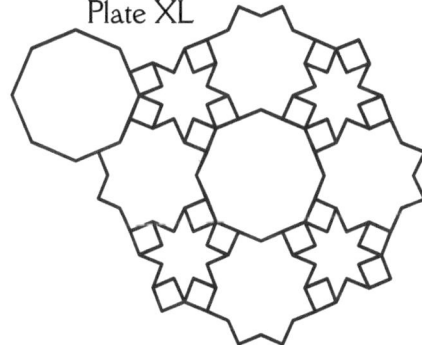

Plate XLI

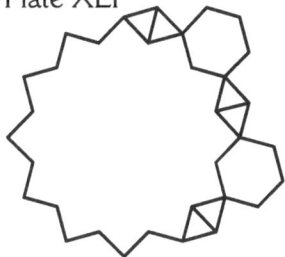

Plate XLII

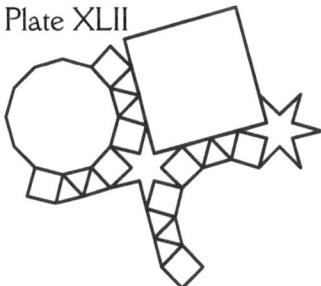

Plate XLIII

This pattern is remarkable because of the eighteen-pointed regular star.

Plate XLIV

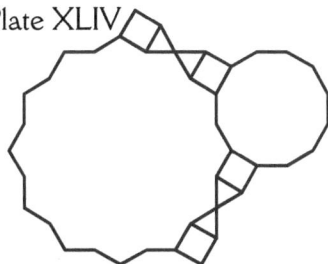

Plate XLV

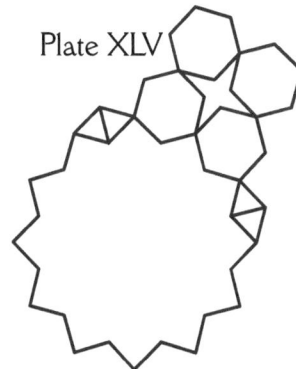

Plate XLVI

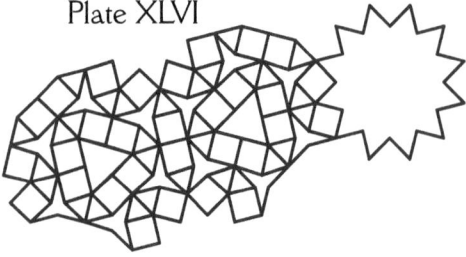

Plate XLVII

Plate XLVIII

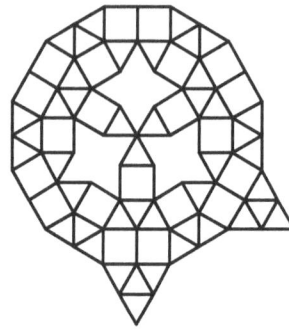

Plate XLIX

Plate L

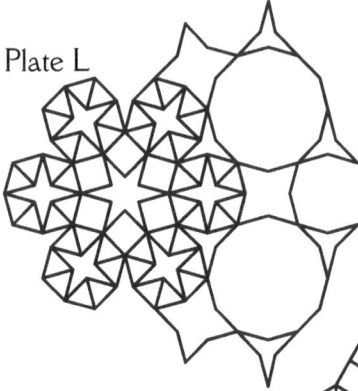

Plate XLVIII shows a nice
possibility for filling in a dodecahedron.

Plate LI

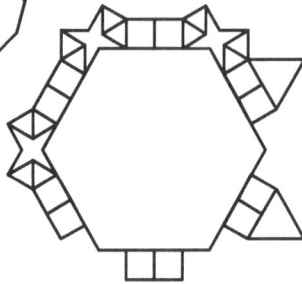

Plate LII

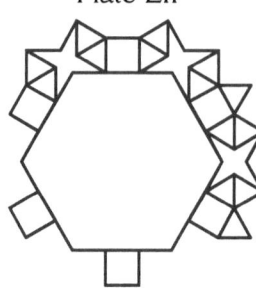

Plate LIII

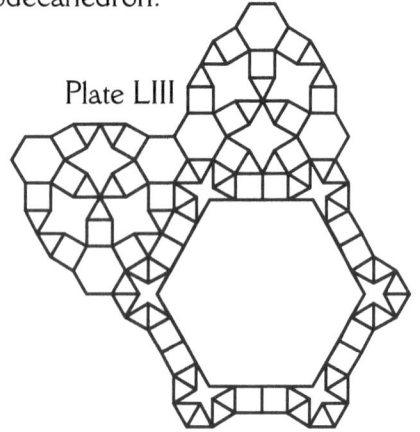

Plate LIV

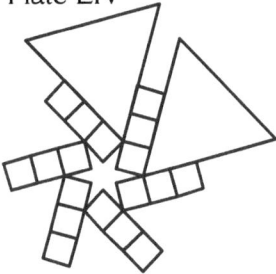

Plate LV

Plate LVI

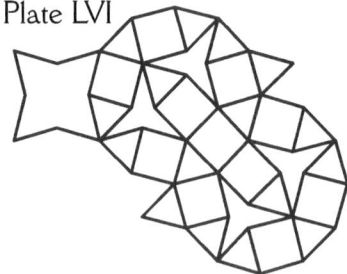

Plate LVII

Plate LVIII

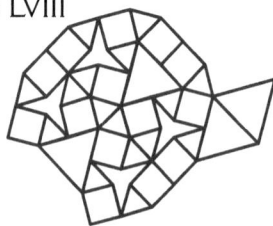

Plate LIX

Plate LX

Plate LXI

Plate LXII

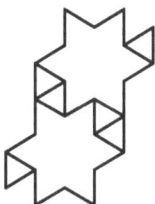

Plate LXIII

The patterns on plate LXI
through LXV were derived one
by one out of the pattern from
the preceding number.

Plate LXIV

Plate LXV

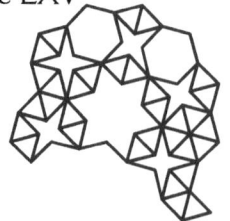

94

Plate LXVI

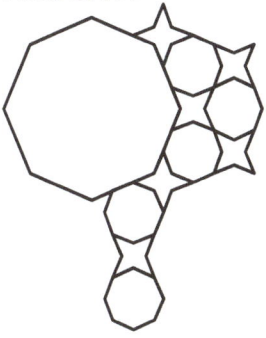

Plate LXVII

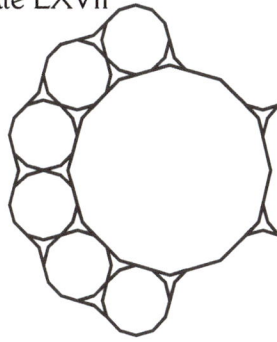

Plate LXVIII

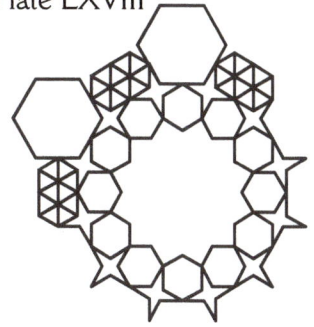

Plate LXIX

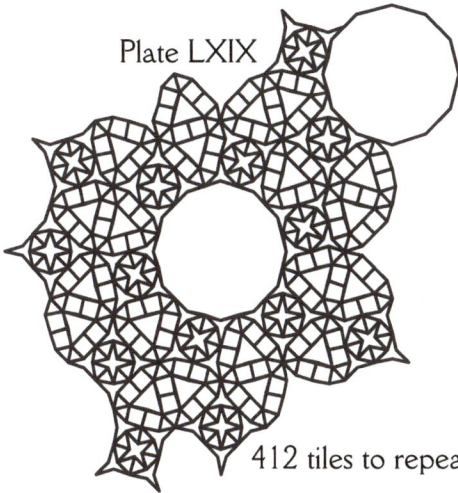

412 tiles to repeat

Plate LXX

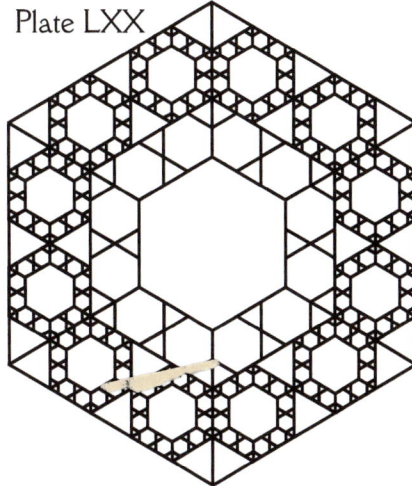

Plate LXXI

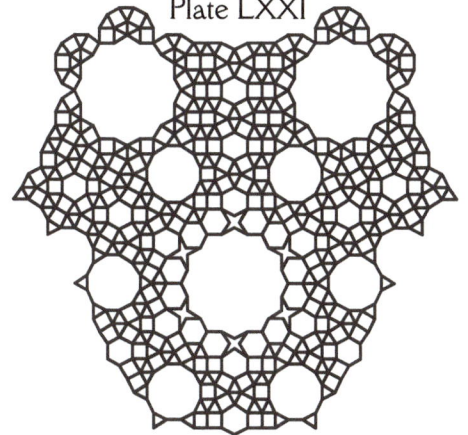

540 parts to repeat

Plate LXXIII

Plate LXIV

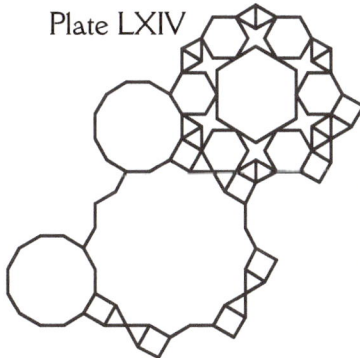

Plate LXXII

Plate LXXVI

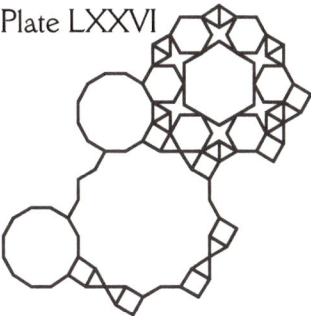

A regular star has two inner angles that alternate. There is a relationship between those two angles. For example, one of the angles of the 4-pointed star in plate LXIII is 30 degrees. The other is then 360-360/4 -30 degree =240 degrees. The 4 comes from the 4-pointed star. In a 6-pointed star with one angle of 30 degrees the other is 360-360/6-30 degrees.

Plate LXXV

Plate LXXVII

Plate LXXVIII

Plate LXXIX

Plate LXXX

Plate LXXXI

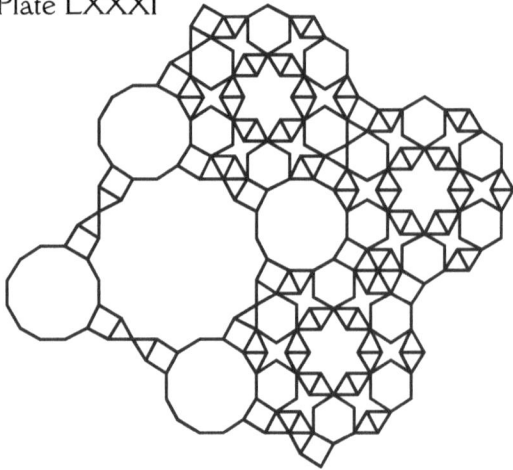

Plate LXXXII

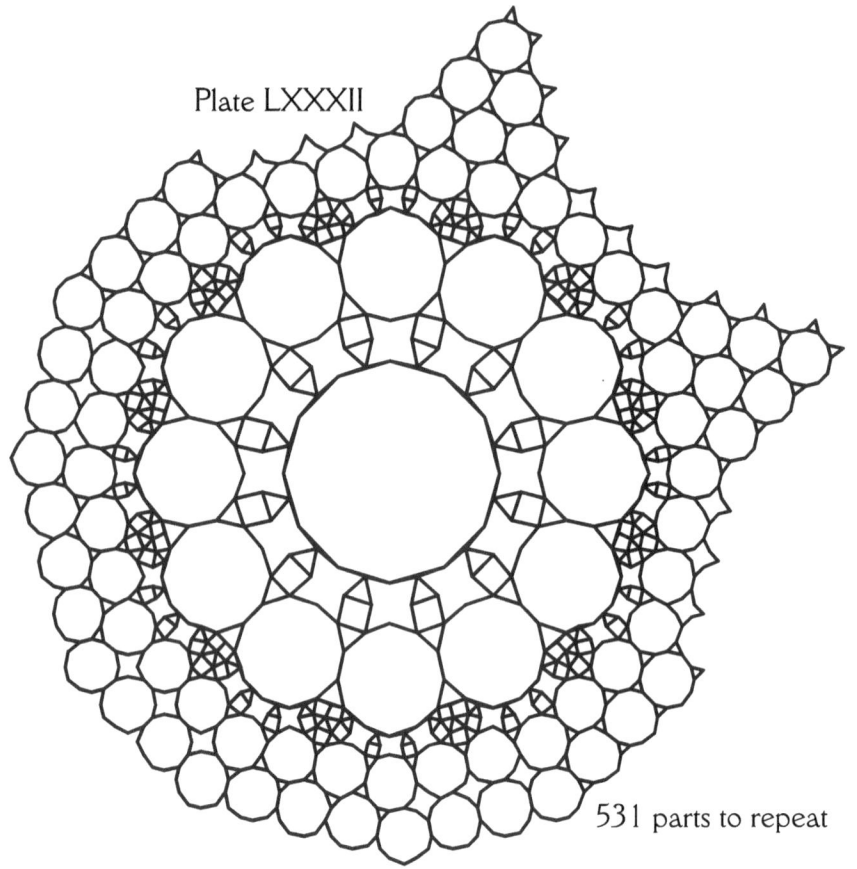

531 parts to repeat

Plate LXXXIII

www.ingramcontent.com/pod-product-compliance
Lightning Source LLC
Chambersburg PA
CBHW060814270326
41930CB00002B/40